AF605673

FESTIVALS, PARTIES AND CELEBRATIONS FROM AROUND THE WORLD

WOODY BRAMBLES

LOUIE & TED

FESTIVALS, PARTIES AND CELEBRATIONS FROM AROUND THE WORLD

It is a fundamental part of human nature to come together with other people. This can be for many reasons. Some events are formal and serious, such as religious ceremonies and funerals. Others are fun and joyous, and filled with energy, such as birthday parties, carnivals and music festivals. In between the serious and joyous are a wide range of different celebrations.

Some celebrations are experienced in many places and at the same time all around the world. Other events take place in small communities and are observed by few people.

Many events are based on customs that go back hundreds of years, with clearly defined traditions and rules as to how they are celebrated.

Some celebrations have travelled far from their original homes, as generations of migrants continue to spread around the world. This has helped create multicultural communities that are more diverse in their ways of bringing people together. Whatever the reason, welcome to the book of *Festivals, Parties and Celebrations from around the World*!

ALBUQUERQUE INTERNATIONAL BALLOON FIESTA

WHERE: **ALBUQUERQUE, UNITED STATES**

WHEN: **FIRST WEEK OF OCTOBER**

The Albuquerque Balloon Fiesta is the largest balloon event in the world. It began in 1972 with just 13 balloons taking part. Since then, the number of participants has grown, with up to 1000 balloons taking to the skies each year along with hundreds of thousands of people turning out to watch.

Aside from the balloons rising together in an enormous group, other activities throughout the festival include the Night Glow (where the balloons are lit up from within at night) and the Special Shape Rodeo.

BUSÓJÁRÁS

WHERE: **MOHÁCS, HUNGARY**

WHEN: **SIX DAYS, USUALLY IN FEBRUARY**

Busójárás, which means Busó-walking, is a traditional celebration held during carnival season in the Hungarian town of Mohács. Men put on horned, wooden masks and sheepskin clothing, then go about the town making noise with cowbells and wooden noisemakers to try to scare winter away. The day ends with the Busó men dancing around a large bonfire in the city square.

Other festivities during Busójárás, which dates back to the 18th century, include masquerades, folk music, parades and dancing.

CHEUNG CHAU BUN FESTIVAL

WHERE: CHEUNG CHAU ISLAND, HONG KONG

WHEN: BASED ON CHINESE CALENDAR; APRIL OR MAY

The Cheung Chau Bun Festival is held every year on the eighth day of the fourth month of the Chinese calendar. It is celebrated with giant papier-mâché statues, parades in which people dress up as heroes and are suspended in the air, and the festival highlight of bun snatching. This is when competitors climb giant towers to retrieve buns; the higher they climb, the more luck they bring their family.

Throughout the festival, tens of thousands of buns are consumed, and for several of the days the entire island of Cheung Chau becomes vegetarian.

UP HELLY AA

WHERE: **SHETLAND ISLANDS, SCOTLAND**

WHEN: **LAST TUESDAY IN JANUARY**

The tradition of Up Helly Aa dates back to the 1880s. It is celebrated at a number of places on the Shetland Islands, with one of the most famous at Lerwick. Up to a thousand men known as guizers dress up in costumes and march towards a Viking longship, which is built just for the festival. Once all the guizers have surrounded the ship, they sing a song before setting it on fire with their torches.

Up Helly Aa, which means 'Up Holy All', takes place in the middle of winter and was traditionally held to mark the end of the Christmas season, known as Yule.

BIRTHDAYS

Around the world there are many ways to celebrate a birthday. For many this involves a birthday party with cake, blowing out the candles, singing songs and playing party games, wearing party hats, putting up decorations and receiving presents from guests.

In some parts of the world birthday traditions are quite different. In Venezuela it is common to have your head pushed into your birthday cake, while in Hungary and Argentina people celebrate by pulling on your earlobes. The popular activity of whacking a sweet-filled piñata until it bursts came originally from China, along with cramming long noodles into your mouth until you can fit no more (this is supposed to bring a long and healthy life). One of the more frightening traditions comes from Switzerland, where parents hire a scary clown to follow you around, teasing and tormenting you before throwing a pie at you for good luck.

Other traditions include birthday bumps (United Kingdom), which is when you are held by your hands and legs and 'bumped' on the ground, having grease smeared on your nose (Canada) and getting coated in flour (Jamaica).

In China, Japan, Vietnam, Mongolia and South Korea, people celebrate their birthdays at the same time in a tradition known as East Asian age reckoning. This is where newborns are considered one year old at birth, and everyone adds a year to their age at the same time (which can be determined by either the Sun, Moon or when New Year's Day is celebrated).

South Koreans also celebrate the first birthday by putting the child in front of a series of objects. Whichever one they grab first is thought to determine what they grow up to be.

ALMABTRIEB

WHERE: ALPINE REGIONS OF EUROPE

WHEN: AUTUMN; SEPTEMBER TO OCTOBER

The celebration of Almabtrieb takes place in the alpine regions of Europe, in countries such as Austria, Germany, Italy and Switzerland. The name means to 'drive from the mountain pasture', and celebrates the return of cattle from the higher alpine pastures to their home stables in the valleys below.

This event takes place in autumn and, while once celebrated by local farmers and villagers, cattle trains have become popular tourist attractions. On return, the cattle are decorated and led through the town before returning to their stables.

SONGKRAN

WHERE: **VARIOUS PARTS OF SOUTH AND SOUTH-EAST ASIA**

WHEN: **APRIL 13–15**

Songkran is a Lunar New Year festival celebrated in many parts of South-East Asia, such as Thailand, Cambodia, Laos, Myanmar, Sri Lanka and parts of Vietnam, India and China.

In Thailand it is one of the most celebrated events of the year. Throughout the festival people return home to visit family, Buddhists visit temples and it is custom to clean your home. Lots of people also celebrate by splashing each other with water, whether it be from a hose, water pistol or bucket.

LA TOMATINA

WHERE: **BUÑOL, SPAIN**

WHEN: **LAST WEDNESDAY IN AUGUST**

La Tomatina is one of the biggest food-fight festivals in the world. Around 20,000 lucky people travel to Buñol to throw over 100 tonnes of over-ripe tomatoes at each other, which by law have to be squashed before being thrown. The fight starts once someone reaches a ham at the top of a greasy wooden pole, and lasts for one hour. After the fight, fire trucks hose the streets of Buñol clean.

Some believe La Tomatina began when two men started throwing tomatoes at the public as an act of political protest. It is held purely for the sake of entertainment.

THAIPUSAM

WHERE: **VARIOUS PARTS OF ASIA; TAMIL COMMUNITIES AROUND THE WORLD**

WHEN: **BASED ON TAMIL CALENDAR; JANUARY OR FEBRUARY**

The festival of Thiaspusam is celebrated by Tamil communities around the world. It honours the Hindu god of war Murugan, son of Shiva and Parvati, who received a spear from Parvati, which he used to defeat the evil demon army of Tarakasura.

Thaipusam is celebrated in a number of ways. Tamils offer fruits and flowers of yellow and orange to Murugan, his favourite colours; they shave their heads before travelling to a temple, sometimes carrying with them milk, water and other tributes in little jugs; while fanatical devotees celebrate by piercing their bodies.

NEW YEAR'S EVE & DAY

Celebrating New Year's Eve (and Day) means different things to different people. For many it is a time to come together with friends and have a party. For adults this can mean drinking, dancing and trying to find someone to kiss at midnight, and ending up with a sore head the next day. For others it is a time for prayer (Muslims) or visiting families, exchanging gifts, buying new clothes and cleaning (Hindus).

When the new year takes place varies, too. For people that follow the Gregorian calendar, New Year's Eve is December 31 and New Year's Day is January 1. In other parts of the world the dates change from year to year, and may be determined by solar, lunar or other calendars.

Common customs around the world include going to public spaces to enjoy music, dancing and 'ringing in the new year' with crowds of people. For some people, the main event is watching enormous firework displays go off as the new year begins. Some people prefer to watch all this happen on television from the safety and comfort of their living room.

In some parts of the world there are different ways to mark

the occasion. In Spain it is tradition to eat 12 grapes from the stroke of midnight, with one grape for every bell strike. This is considered to bring a year of good luck. People in Denmark jump off chairs just before midnight to leave evil spirits behind in the old year.

In Scotland and parts of England is the custom of first-footing. This tradition believes the first person to enter your home in the new year should be male, tall and have dark hair, which leads to good luck for the coming year. Similar traditions exist in Greece and Georgia.

DIWALI

WHERE: INDIA, NEPAL AND AROUND THE WORLD

WHEN: BASED ON HINDU CALENDAR; OCTOBER OR NOVEMBER

Diwali, also known as The Festival of Lights, is a popular Hindu festival celebrated in many parts of the world, particularly in India and Nepal. It runs for five days and means different things to different cultures, though in essence it celebrates the victories of light over darkness, knowledge over ignorance and good over evil.

Common Diwali traditions include cleaning and decorating one's home, wearing new clothes, giving gifts to family, decorating homes and other buildings with fancy lights and candles, drawing rangolis and enjoying fireworks.

PALIO DI SIENA

WHERE: **SIENA, ITALY**

WHEN: **JULY 2 AND AUGUST 16**

The Palio di Siena are twice-yearly horse races that date back to 1656. Before each race is the Corteo Storico, where people parade in historical costumes.

Ten riders on bare horseback compete in each race, wearing the colours of their local Siena district. They race around the town square three times, with many riders falling off before the finish line. The winner receives a banner and bragging rights for their district, while the district that is the longest without a win is nicknamed *nonna*, which means grandmother.

LOI KRATHONG & YI PENG

WHERE: **SOUTH-EAST ASIA**

WHEN: **BASED ON THAI CALENDAR; USUALLY IN NOVEMBER**

People celebrate Loi Krathong by placing a krathong – a beautifully decorated basket made from folded banana leaves and containing incense, candles and coins – into a river on the night of a full Moon, usually in November. As they let their krathong go, they make a wish.

At around the same time is the Thai festival of Yi Peng. During this celebration, homes and streets are decorated with beautiful paper lanterns, while at night thousands of lanterns are released into the sky in honour of Buddha.

WHERE: PAMPLONA, SPAIN

WHEN: FROM MIDDAY JULY 6 TO MIDNIGHT JULY 14

San Fermín is one of the most popular festivals in Spain. The week-long celebrations begin with fireworks at city hall, then the next day a procession in which dancers, street performers and crowds follow a statue of Saint Fermín.

Other events include the Giants and Big-heads parade, fireworks displays and bullfights. For the adventurous there is the daily running of the bulls, in which a dozen bulls and steers chase people down the streets towards the Pamplona bullring. Every year there are many injuries and sometimes even deaths.

FILM & FASHION

Film festivals are held all around the world. They take place in the biggest cities and the smallest country towns. They can be organised by genre (such as comedy, horror or western film festivals), where they were made (such as African, Korean or French film festivals) and who made them.

Some film festivals play a big role in how successful a movie becomes. Winning an award at the Sundance, Toronto or Cannes Film Festivals can make a huge difference to the amount of money a movie ends up making.

Film festivals are also important as a form of advertising. Celebrity actors, actresses and filmmakers turn out for the fans and photographers on the red carpet, wearing glamorous clothing and creating a sense of 'Hollywood' buzz for their films. They give interviews to journalists who then promote their movies in newspapers, on television and online. Movies and their cast and crew may end up going to lots of festivals as part of their promotional tour.

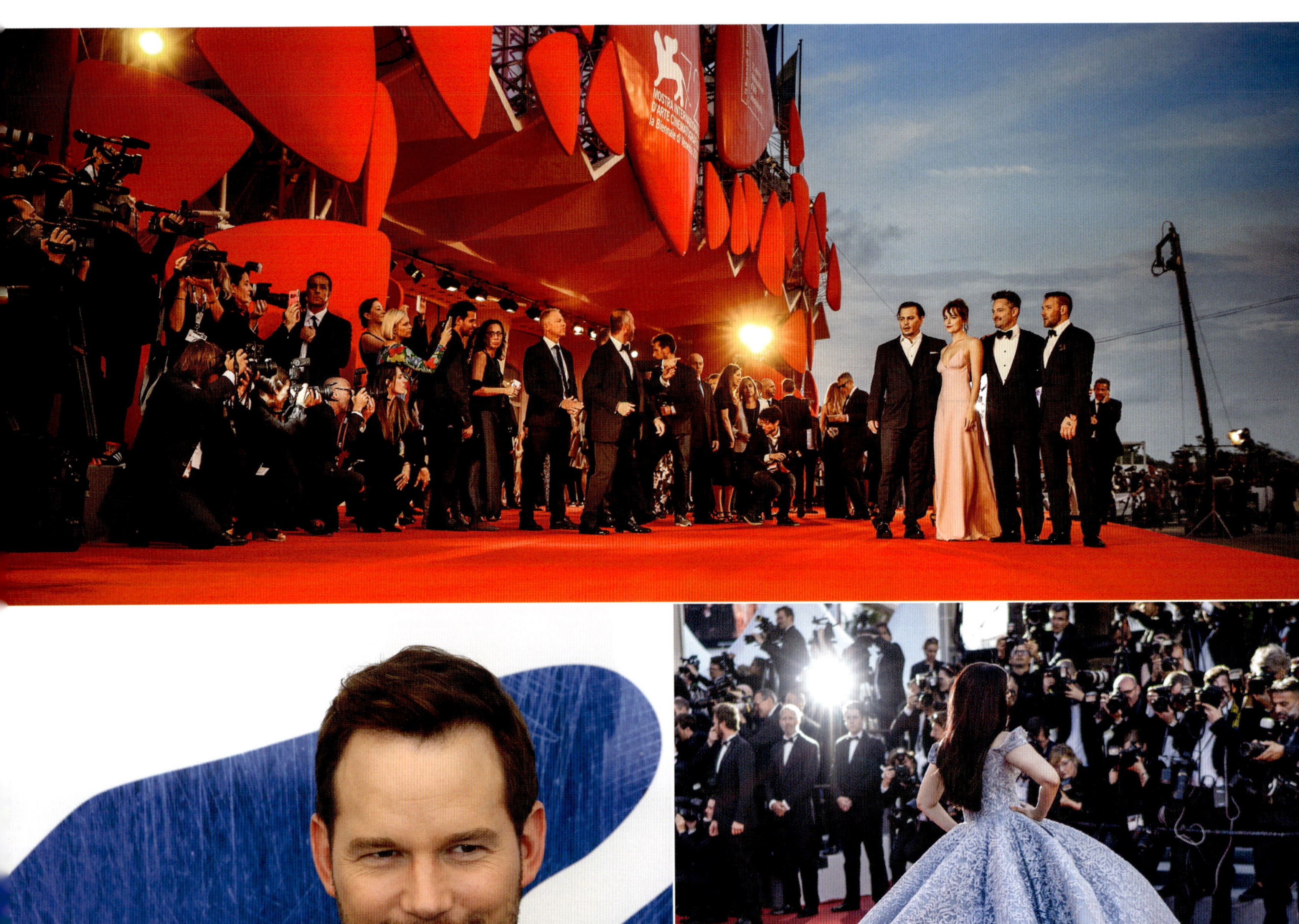

Fashion festivals are held to showcase fashion designers and their latest outfits. These festivals are held every year and in the world's biggest cities. Some of the most famous include Paris, Berlin, London and New York.

Male and female models wear a range of clothes – from swimwear to formal, and often outfits that appear quite unusual – and parade them up and down a long walkway in front of crowds of people. Backstage is a hive of activity as models, makeup artists and various other people work behind the scenes to keep the festival running.

BORYEONG MUD FESTIVAL

WHERE: **BORYEONG, SOUTH KOREA**

WHEN: **APPROXIMATELY TWO WEEKS IN EARLY JULY**

This festival attracts thousands of visitors every summer to the beachside city of Boryeong. In the 1990s, Boryeong became famous for its nearby mud flats and the vitamin-rich cosmetics they created. In order to promote the cosmetics, the Boryeong Mud Festival was born.

Main attractions throughout the festivities include a mud pool, mud slide, giant mud bath, mud maze and mud body painting, along with a series of music events and fireworks displays.

COOPER'S HILL CHEESE-ROLLING

WHERE: **COOPER'S HILL, ENGLAND**

WHEN: **LAST MONDAY IN MAY**

This unusual festival takes place near the English village of Brockworth. A wheel of cheese is rolled from the top of Cooper's Hill, after which competitors chase after it. The winner is the first person to cross the line at the bottom of the hill.

The cheese can reach speeds of over 100 kilometres, and every year there are numerous injuries to competitors. That hasn't stopped this event from becoming increasingly popular. Originally held for the Brockworth locals, the race has been won by competitors from America, Australia, Nepal, New Zealand and Wales.

WHERE:	**INDIA, NEPAL AND AROUND THE WORLD**	Holi, also known as The Festival of Colours, is a popular festival observed by Hindu communities around the world. It runs for a night and a day, and celebrates the beginning of spring and the triumph of good over evil.
WHEN:	**BASED ON HINDU CALENDAR; FEBRUARY OR MARCH**	The day before Holi begins, bonfires are lit to celebrate burning Holika (the devil). The next morning people throw coloured powder at each other, and anyone is fair game. Later in the day, people share food and drinks with family and friends, such as guija (dumplings), mathri (flaky biscuits) and malpua (pancakes).

MONKEY BUFFET FESTIVAL

WHERE: **LOPBURI, THAILAND**

WHEN: **LAST SUNDAY IN NOVEMBER**

The Monkey Buffet Festival is an annual celebration held in honour of the thousands of local monkeys, and is put on by the city of Lopburi as a way of thanking them for bringing tourists to the area.

Close to 4000 kilograms of fruit, vegetables, cakes and sweet drinks are offered to the monkeys. Some of these treats are laid out on tables or piled into pyramids, while others are frozen in blocks of ice for the monkeys to lick.

EASTER

Easter is a time of year that many people look forward to. For children it can mean a visit from the Easter bunny and eating lots of chocolate, while for many it is an opportunity to come together and celebrate with family.

This Christian religious festival celebrates the resurrection of Jesus Christ from the dead. The week leading up to Easter Sunday is filled with a range of holy days and traditions, often in the form of prayer and church worship. The exact dates for Easter change from year to year, though its celebrations take place sometime in March, April or May.

Aside from religious customs, many people celebrate Easter by decorating and hiding eggs (real, chocolate or plastic) around the house and garden for children to hunt and find, and by giving loved ones gifts of chocolate. The figure of the Easter bunny is common in many parts of the world, though some in Australia prefer the Easter bilby, as the common rabbit is considered a pest animal.

Other Easter traditions around the world include flying kites and eating hot cross buns and codfish cakes (though not at the same time), which happens on Good Friday in Bermuda.

In parts of Europe people welcome spring by chasing away the darkness of winter with large bonfires.

In Sweden it is common for children to dress up as Easter witches, wearing tatty clothes, headscarves and face paint. They then make their way from house to house, offering their neighbours drawings or other gifts in exchange for sweets.

BATTLE OF THE ORANGES

WHERE: IVREA, ITALY

WHEN: FROM SUNDAY TO TUESDAY, 40 DAYS BEFORE EASTER

While its origins are unclear, a common story tells of a young miller's daughter named Violetta, who fought and killed an evil marquis trying to harm her. For the people of Ivrea this was a symbolic moment of liberation.

Thousands take part in the fight in one of nine teams, with each team wearing unique colours. Members of these teams throw oranges at the 'henchmen' of the evil marquis, who ride in horse-drawn carts. The battle is fierce and injuries are common. Over 200,000 kilograms of oranges are used during the festival.

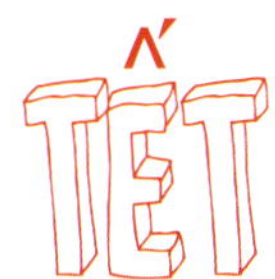

WHERE: VIETNAM; VIETNAMESE COMMUNITIES AROUND THE WORLD

WHEN: BASED ON LUNAR CALENDAR; JANUARY OR FEBRUARY

This festival is also known as Vietnamese New Year, and is considered the most important celebration in Vietnamese culture. It is celebrated in many ways.

On the first day, it is custom to spend time with immediate family. Children give their elders traditional greetings, and in return elders give them red envelopes of money. People often clean and decorate their houses, often with a bamboo pole called a cay neu. People parade in the streets and make as much noise as possible with fireworks, drums and lion dancing, which chases away evil spirits.

ELS ENFARINATS

WHERE: **IBI, SPAIN**

WHEN: **DECEMBER 28**

Also known as the Battle of Enfarinats, this celebration sees two groups fight each other with eggs, flour and firecrackers in a tradition over 200 years old.

On one side are the ‘Els Enfarinats’ and on the other are the ‘La Oposicio’. In the morning the first group take over the town, making up terrible new laws, giving out fines and sending people to ‘jail’, while the second group are responsible for fighting back. The day of festivities ends with order restored and any money collected in fines is donated to charity.

RAMADAN

WHERE: **IN MUSLIM COMMUNITIES AROUND THE WORLD**

WHEN: **BASED ON ISLAMIC LUNAR CALENDAR; MAY TO JUNE**

Ramadan is the ninth month of the Islamic calendar. It is an important time for Muslims, and considered one of the Five Pillars of Islam.

Muslims say additional prayers, attend mosques and read the Quran during Ramadan. Most people also refrain from eating between dawn and sunset. The meal before sunrise is called suhur, while the meal after sunset is called iftar and usually includes dates. At the end of Ramadan is the celebration Eid-al-Fitr: 'Feast of Breaking the Fast'.

CHRISTMAS

Christmas is a time of year that many people look forward to. For children in the Southern Hemisphere it means summer holidays and time off school, along with presents and (hopefully) a visit from Santa Claus. For adults it means extra days off work, a chance to catch up with friends and family, and an opportunity to indulge in a Christmas feast.

In most countries, Christmas Day is celebrated on December 25. However, several dates in January are also celebrated, particularly by members of several Eastern European churches.

Christmas is a Christian festival that celebrates the birth of Jesus Christ, and traditionally lasts for 12 days.

People around the world celebrate Christmas in contrasting ways. In the Northern Hemisphere, it takes place during the middle of winter. This means there is snow and it is very cold. In many cities there are Christmas markets, with fairground rides, seasonal foods and opportunities to visit Santa. In the Southern Hemisphere, however, it is the middle of summer. People go swimming at the beach and generally try to escape the heat.

Other popular Christmas traditions include decorating your house with fairy lights and other decorations, along with a Christmas tree with lots of presents underneath. In the Philippines the payol, or star-shaped lantern, is just as important as a tree. Some also hang up a stocking by the fireplace, so that Santa can leave behind some presents.

Nativity scenes showing the birth of Jesus in Bethlehem are also common, as well as a Christmas lunch or dinner of roast turkey, ham and all the trimmings. An after-lunch nap is also strongly recommended.

DÍA DE MUERTOS

WHERE: MEXICO; MEXICAN COMMUNITIES AROUND THE WORLD

WHEN: OCTOBER 31 TO NOVEMBER 2

Day of the Dead is in fact a three-day celebration. It begins with All Hallow's Eve (Halloween), then All Saint's Day and finishes with All Soul's Day.

Families observe numerous customs. They visit cemeteries to tidy up the graves of their ancestors, and also to build them altars with offerings of food, drink and other decorations. Shrines may also be built at home and include marigold flowers, muertos ('bread of the dead') and sugar skulls. Skulls and skeletons are a common symbol of the festival, especially during the Day of the Dead parades.

OKTOBERFEST

WHERE: **MUNICH, GERMANY**

WHEN: **SEPTEMBER TO OCTOBER**

Oktoberfest, the world's largest beer festival, began in 1811. In the early years there were horse races, an agricultural show and carousel rides, along with beer stands that soon became very popular.

Today, close to six million people attend Oktoberfest each year. Major attractions include drinking in the beer halls, eating traditional foods like würstl (sausage), schweinebraten (roast pork) and brazen (pretzels), and dressing in traditional clothing like lederhosen (leather shorts) and dirndls (traditional dresses).

WHITE NIGHTS FESTIVAL

WHERE: **SAINT PETERSBURG, RUSSIA**

WHEN: **MAY TO JULY**

The Russian city of Saint Petersburg is famous for having almost round-the-clock daylight during the summer months. These 'white nights' led to the creation of their White Nights Festival, which runs from May to July.

Highlights include ballet, opera and music events, along with a series of carnivals recreating different periods of Russian history. The most popular event is the Scarlet Sails celebration of a red-sailed ship and spectacular fireworks display. This event marks the end of the school year and is attended by millions.

BURNING MAN FESTIVAL

WHERE: **BLACK ROCK DESERT, UNITED STATES**

WHEN: **LAST SUNDAY IN AUGUST TO FIRST MONDAY IN SEPTEMBER**

Burning Man is held in the windy Black Rock Desert, in the temporary town of Black Rock City, which disappears once the festival is over. It began in 1986 with just 20 participants, and is now attended by close to 50,000 people each year.

'Burners' are encouraged to live by a set of rules that help them get the most out of the festival. This includes being self-reliant, helping each other, giving gifts and leaving no trace. There are art installations all around Black Rock City, and the festival ends with the burning of an enormous wooden man.

MUSIC

Music festivals are popular around the world. There are festivals dedicated to nearly all genres of music, including rock, classical, pop, opera and hip-hop to name just a few. Some festivals combine many of these genres together, and can take place on a single stage for just a day or on many stages over the course of a week (or even longer).

In recent years music festivals have become more popular, especially with young adults. They see it is a rite of passage to travel the globe and attend the biggest and best music festivals once they finish school. Some of the most famous festivals include Glastonbury (England), Roskilde (Denmark), Coachella (United States) and Fuji Rock (Japan). Large events like these offer camping grounds for people to stay in for the duration of the festival.

While the main attraction is music, most festivals offer other events and activities to keep people entertained. This can include art displays, movie screenings, stand-up comedy and carnival rides. Some people like to bring their own entertainment and perform for passers-by. This can include fire twirling, which is similar to the Maori tradition of poi.

INTERNATIONAL SAND SCULPTURE FESTIVAL

WHERE: **PÊRA, PORTUGAL**

WHEN: **APRIL TO OCTOBER**

This festival claims to be the biggest sand sculpture event in the world. Each year there is a different theme, which in the past has included Hollywood Films and Characters, Animal Kingdom and Mythology. The event takes place in Sand City on close to four acres of land.

Around 50 sculptors from around the world take part in the festival, using close to 40,000 tonnes of sand to make their works of art. Some of the sculptures are up to 12 metres tall, and are able to be viewed by the public for up to seven months.

HARBIN INTERNATIONAL ICE AND SNOW SCULPTURE FESTIVAL

WHERE: **HARBIN, CHINA**

WHEN: **JANUARY TO FEBRUARY**

The Harbin Ice and Snow Sculpture Festival is a major attraction popular with people from around the world, with up to 15 million visitors each year. As many as 10,000 workers are needed to cut the ice blocks used to build the event.

Zhaolin Park mostly contains ice sculptures of animals and other characters popular with children, while Sun Island has a range of enormous snow sculptures that can only be seen during the day. Ice and Snow World has enormous ice sculptures that are lit up at night, with some of them close to 50 metres tall.

SETSUBUN

WHERE: **JAPAN**

WHEN: **FEBRUARY 3 OR 4**

Setsubun is celebrated the day before spring begins. Families throw roasted soybeans out the door of their home or at a member of the family wearing an oni mask. Oni are a type of demon spirit that bring bad luck. Throwing soybeans chases evil from the home and brings good luck for the coming year.

Other customs include eating soybeans (one for each year of your life plus one) and an entire sushi roll in silence while facing a lucky direction. In some places celebrities throw packets of soybeans to thousands of eager fans.

WHERE: **VALENCIA, SPAIN**

WHEN: **MARCH 15–19**

The festival of Falles is held in honour of Saint Joseph. Throughout the festival locals wear traditional clothing and take part in many events that make this one of Spain's most popular celebrations. These include La Despertà (an early morning wake-up from brass bands and firecrackers), La Mascletà (daily fireworks), L'Ofrena de flors (offering of flowers to the Virgin Mary) and Els Castells and La Nit del Foc (more fireworks). On each day of the festival are parades of giant puppets called falles, which on the final night are loaded with firecrackers and set alight during La Cremà ('the burning'). If you like fire, this festival may be for you.

CALENDAR HOLIDAYS

Every country in the world observes particular dates as holidays. Examples of shared holidays in Australia and New Zealand include Good Friday, Easter Monday, Anzac Day, Christmas Day and Boxing Day. All of these are public holidays, which means they are observed across the country and cause schools and most workplaces to close down for the day. These holidays also come with a range of traditions and customs, some of which are centuries old.

However, some calendar 'holidays' are completely made-up. This is not to say they don't serve a valuable purpose: some made-up holidays help to spread awareness of social causes that are very important. Other made-up holidays are purely for the sake of celebrating something fun.

These types of holiday are not officially recognised and do not give people the right to take a day off work or school. These holidays may be observed in just one country, while others have caught on around the world and are observed in lots of places. The following examples are just a tiny selection of the weird and unusual ways some people choose to celebrate the calendar days of the year.

January 12 is Kiss A Ginger Day, while January 14 is known as Dress Up Your Pet Day.

If ice-cream is your thing then get excited for the first Saturday in February, as this is Ice-cream for Breakfast Day. Later that month is Wave at Your Neighbour Day (February 7), though in Australia Neighbour's Day is celebrated on the last Sunday in March.

May 4 is now Star Wars Day ('May the *fourth* be with you'), while the first Sunday in May is time to bust a gut for World Laughter Day. You should give your cat a cuddle on June 4 as this is Hug Your Cat Day, though be careful what you do on June 18 as this is both International **Picnic** Day and International **Panic** Day.

For the salty dogs out there, September 19 is Talk Like a Pirate Day, while October 20 is International Sloth Day.

DUANWU FESTIVAL

WHERE: CHINA

WHEN: BASED ON CHINESE CALENDAR; MAY OR JUNE

In Western countries Duanwu is more commonly known as the Dragon Boat Festival. It was originally celebrated in China, and today is celebrated in many parts of the world. It takes place on the fifth day of the fifth month of the Chinese calendar, the exact date of which changes from year to year.

People celebrate Duanwu by eating zongzi, a type of dumpling, drinking wine and watching dragon boat races. Each boat traditionally has 20 paddlers, one steerer and a drummer, with races typically being a frantic sprint over 500 metres.

CORREFOC

WHERE: **CATALONIA, SPAIN**

WHEN: **VARIOUS TIMES**

The word *correfoc* means 'fire-run'. Participants in correfocs dress up as devils or monsters and attach fireworks to their costumes, or carry pitchforks and other items and attach fireworks to these. The fireworks are then lit and the devils run through crowds of onlookers. Members of the crowd try to get as close to the devils as possible, and wear protective clothing to stop them from getting burnt.

Correfocs are popular in Catalonian festivals, and are believed to have evolved from the centuries-old medieval tradition of ball de diables ('devil-dances').

KANDY ESALA PERAHERA

WHERE: **KANDY, SRI LANKA**

WHEN: **JULY OR AUGUST**

This important Sri Lankan festival is famous for its processions of dancers, jugglers, fire-breathers, musicians and elephants. The festival goes back many centuries, and first came about as a way of asking the gods for rain. Later it was used as a way of honouring the Sacred Tooth Relic of Buddha. That is why this festival is also known as the Festival of the Tooth.

At the front of the procession is a beautifully decorated elephant known as a tusker, which carries a casket containing a substitute for the Sacred Tooth Relic.

GUY FAWKES NIGHT

WHERE: GREAT BRITAIN AND AROUND THE WORLD

WHEN: NOVEMBER 5

Also known as Bonfire or Firework Night, Guy Fawkes is a popular British event celebrating the failed plot to kill King James I in 1605. Fawkes was arrested while guarding the explosives that had been placed underneath the House of Lords.

Today, Guy Fawkes is mostly observed in Great Britain, where people light bonfires, set off firecrackers or watch huge firework displays. In towns like Ottery is the tradition of tar barrelling, in which local men, women and children hold flaming barrels above their heads as they walk through the streets.

CARNIVALS

Carnivals are famous the world over for being loud and energetic displays of dancing, singing, music and wild street partying. They can involve thousands of participants and hundreds of thousands of spectators, and often involve the wearing of costumes and masks. They take place in many countries and can sometimes last for as long as a month.

The history of carnivals comes from Christianity, and they were a way of celebrating before undertaking the serious period of Lent. Before Lent it was common for people to give up animal products such as dairy and meat, which is where carnivals get their name – the Italian word 'carnevale' means 'to remove meat'. This explains why carnivals can be so wild; people are trying to have fun while they still can!

There are many famous carnivals around the world. Perhaps none are more famous than the Carnival of Rio de Janeiro, Brazil. It is the biggest carnival on the planet, and is famous for having enormous parades, floats and close to 200 samba schools of dancers dressed in flamboyant costumes.

The Carnaval de Oruro, Bolivia, is famous for its folk

dancers, and has close to 40,000 participants taking part, while Barranquilla's Carnival in Colombia is believed to be the second biggest in the world.

The Carnival of Venice, Italy, dates back to the 13th century, and is famous for the masks that people wear. Some of these include the Colombina (half-mask covering the eyes) and Medico Della Peste (plague doctor). In Belgium is the Carnival of Binche, which is famous for its Gilles, which are men in masks and feathered hats. Being made a Gilles is considered to be a great honour.

HALLOWEEN

WHERE: **AROUND THE WORLD**

WHEN: **OCTOBER 31**

Halloween has become popular around the world. For many it is an excuse to have a party, cover your house with frightening decorations, dress up in costumes (which can range from cute-and-cuddly to downright scary) and go trick-or-treating for sweets, and playing party games like apple bobbing.

There are many other traditions associated with Halloween. People carve pumpkins into jack-o-lanterns, placing a candle inside so that they come alive and scare off evil spirits, while placing candles at gravesites is also common.

CASTELL

WHERE: **CATALONIA, SPAIN**

WHEN: **VARIOUS TIMES**

Castells are a popular feature of Catalonian festivals. These tall towers made and dismantled by teams of people have been around for close to 300 years.

At the bottom is the pinya (base), fixing the tower to the ground and providing a 'mattress' for the upper layers to fall onto. Further up are the foire and manilles (additional bases), followed by the tronc (trunk). These are the narrow layers of the castell. The top three layers are the pom de dalt (top of the tower), which are usually children. A castell is only complete once the top child raises four fingers.

INTI RAYMI

WHERE: CUSCO, PERU

WHEN: END OF JUNE

Inti Raymi was an important festival to the Incas that celebrated the sun god Inti. It takes place at the Fortress of Sacsayhuaman and various other parts of Cusco.

Incan celebrations during Inti Raymi included fasting for of a number of days to become 'pure', drinking a special corn-based drink, dancing and music, painting your face, wearing a deer's head and even sacrificing children to the gods. Today, celebrations are mostly to do with music and dancing, colourful costumes and a procession that goes from the Qoricancha (Temple of the Sun) to Sacsayhuaman.

DUCASSE DE MONS

WHERE: **MONS, BELGIUM**

WHEN: **TRINITY SUNDAY**

The festival Ducasse de Mons is made up of two main parts: the procession of Waltrude's Shrine and the battle between Saint George and the dragon.

During the procession, the shrine is carried on a cart pulled by horses, and at one point has to go up a steep hill. If it doesn't make it up in one go, bad luck follows. This has happened three times, in the years before the French Revolution and World Wars I and II. Meanwhile, the public are encouraged to help Saint George fight against the dragon, which is eventually killed by Saint George with a pistol.

WORLD BUSKERS FESTIVAL

WHERE: CHRISTCHURCH, NEW ZEALAND

WHEN: JANUARY

Street performers from around the world come to Christchurch to perform acts of entertainment. This can range from singing and dancing to magic and mime; acrobatics and juggling to comedy and clowning.

PROCESSIONAL GIANTS

WHERE: BELGIUM AND FRANCE

WHEN: VARIOUS TIMES

Throughout Belgium and France are thousands of giant statues used in numerous local festivals. They can represent real or make-believe characters, with some figures first appearing close to 600 years ago.

WHITTLESEA STRAW BEAR

WHERE: WHITTLESEA, ENGLAND

WHEN: SECOND WEEKEND IN JANUARY

An old custom that was brought back in the 1980s by the residents of Whittlesea, in which a man or boy (or both) are covered in straw and led by a 'keeper' from house to house. Musicians play a tune for the bear, who then dances in exchange for gifts.

EL COLACHO

WHERE: CASTRILLO DE MURCIA, SPAIN

WHEN: 60 DAYS AFTER EASTER; JUNE

Also known as baby jumping, this celebration dates back to 1620. Men dress up as devils in red and yellow suits and leap over babies born in the previous year, who are laid on mattresses in the street. This custom is believed to cleanse the children of sin.

WHERE: ALICE SPRINGS, AUSTRALIA

WHEN: SEPTEMBER

This annual boat race is held in the dry river bed of Todd River. Metal boat frames are carried by competitors around the sandy course. It is reportedly the only race of its kind in the world, and was once called off due to wet weather.

WHERE: OAXACA, MEXICO

WHEN: DECEMBER 23

The Night of the Radishes is an annual festival held in Oaxaca, Mexico. Farmers used to decorate their market stalls with carved radishes as a way of attracting customers. They soon became popular as table decorations at Christmas time, and in 1897 Oaxaca held its first radish carving festival.

KONAKI SUMO

WHERE: VARIOUS PARTS OF JAPAN

WHEN: VARIOUS TIMES

Known as the 'crying sumo' festival, sumo wrestlers face off against each other while each holds a baby. The first baby to cry is the winner, while the babies' cries are considered good luck as they frighten away evil spirits. The origins of the festival come from the Japanese proverb: 'Crying babies grow fat.'

WHERE: VARIOUS PARTS OF EUROPE

WHEN: DECEMBER 5

The demon known as Krampus is like an anti-Santa Claus. Where the latter gives children who have been good wonderful presents, Krampus punishes naughty children. Krampusnacht is the night he goes to work, and is celebrated in countries like Austria, Croatia, Hungary, Slovenia and the United States.

WHERE: BRUSSELS, BELGIUM

WHEN: EVERY SECOND YEAR; AUGUST

The Flower Carpet happens once every two years. It takes 100 people four hours to put together, and is made entirely out of begonias. It is made in the Grand Place – the central square of Brussels – and covers an area of about 1800 square metres. At 300 flowers per square metre, that amounts to about 600,000 flowers!

GROUNDHOG DAY

WHERE: UNITED STATES, CANADA AND GERMANY

WHEN: FEBRUARY 2

Belief in Groundhog Day comes from German settlers living in the United States. They believed a sunny day on February 2 meant a groundhog would see its shadow and retreat to its burrow. This in turn meant winter would continue for several weeks. However, if it was a cloudy day then spring would begin early.

WHERE: PIORNAL, SPAIN

WHEN: JANUARY 19–20

During the San Sebastián Festival, the town of Piornal is home to the celebration of Jarramplas. In it, a person wears an armoured suit covered in colourful ribbons, and a horned mask. They walk the streets beating a drum, inviting townspeople to come out and throw turnips at them with great violence.

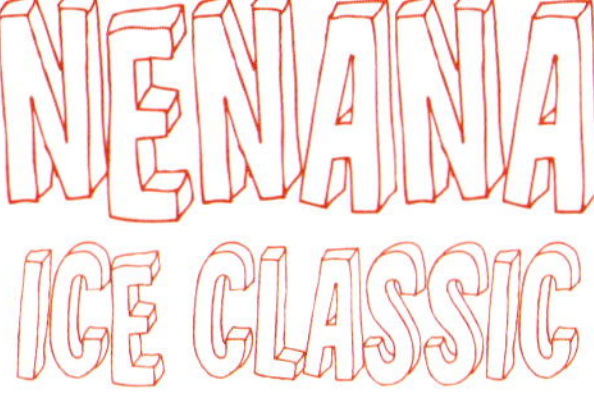

WHERE: NENANA, UNITED STATES

WHEN: WINTER AND ONWARDS

The Nenana Ice Classic is an annual fundraising event in Alaska. A triangular structure is placed on the frozen Tanana River, with people buying tickets and guessing when they think the ice will break and the structure will fall into the water. Since it began in 1906, over 10 million dollars has been raised for charity.

First published in 2017 by
louie & ted
54A Alexandra Parade
Clifton Hill Vic 3068
Australia
+61 3 9419 9406
dog@wdog.com.au
wdog.com.au

Printed and bound in China by 1010 Printing International

National Library of Australia
Cataloguing-in-Publication data:
Creator: Brambles, Woody.
Title: Festivals, Parties and Celebrations from
around the World.
ISBN: 9781742034713 (pbk)
Target Audience: For primary school age.
Subjects: Festivals--Juvenile literature.
Parties--Juvenile literature.
Anniversaries--Juvenile literature.

louie & ted would like to thank Neil Conning for his careful and thorough proofreading.

10 9 8 7 6 5 4 3 2 1   17 18 19 20 21